Christmas 1

Twelve Poems for Those We Love

ex libris

Candlestick Press

Published by:

Candlestick Press,
Diversity House, 72 Nottingham Road, Arnold, Nottingham NG5 6LF
www.candlestickpress.co.uk

Design and typesetting by Craig Twigg

Printed by Ratcliff & Roper Print Group, Nottinghamshire, UK

Cover illustration © Hilke MacIntyre, 2021
www.macintyre-art.com

Candlestick Press monogram © Barbara Shaw, 2008

Donation to Our Dementia Choir
www.ourdementiachoir.com

ISBN 978 1 913627 02 7

Acknowledgements

The poems in this pamphlet are reprinted from the following books, all by
permission of the publishers listed unless stated otherwise. Every effort has been
made to trace the copyright holders of the poems published in this book. The
editor and publisher apologise if any material has been included without
permission or without the appropriate acknowledgement, and would be glad to be
told of anyone who has not been consulted.

Thanks are due to all the copyright holders cited below for their kind permission:

Kate Bass, *The North* (Issue 36. 2005) by kind permission of Smith/Doorstop on
behalf of the author; UA Fanthorpe, *Christmas Poems* (Enitharmon Press, 2002);
Nathalie Handal, *Black Renaissance*, Winter/Spring 2012; 11, 2/3; Literature
Online by permission of University of Pittsburgh Press; WS Merwin, *Selected
Poems* (Bloodaxe Books, 2007) www.bloodaxebooks.com; Maureen Richardson,
first published here by kind permission of Helen O'Connell and family.

Thanks are also due to the authors listed below for kind permission to use their
poems, all of which are published here for the first time:

Bill Adair, Christina Buckton, Jeanette Burton, Tony Curtis, Robert Hamberger,
Corinna Keefe and Lorraine Mariner.

All permissions cleared courtesy of Swift Permissions
swiftpermissions@gmail.com

Where poets are no longer living, their dates are given.

Contents

The Walk to Windy Nook

Out at Christmastime we'll go
Walking through bright fields of snow
Where there grows no grass at all.
Where the top of every wall,
Every fence, every tree,
Gleams diamond white – as white can be.
While dragon-breath dense clouds surround
Young owners of such gleeful sounds,
Pointing out the way we came,
Never one of them the same,
All across the fields there'll be
Arrows of silver filigree.
And our mothers always know
By small footprints in the snow
Where it is we children go....

Maureen Richardson (1943 – 2020)

A Child's Prayer at Christmas

Let us remember the small child
who, when asked by her grandmother
what she wanted for Christmas,
said, "A camel."
You mean a puppy?
"No, a camel,
and I need it before Christmas.
I want to follow the star to Bethlehem.
I want to ask Jesus to be my brother."

"But he's already like a brother,"
her grandmother said,
"We celebrate his birthday every Christmas
and give him praise all through the year."
"I am not looking for that type of brother.
I want the one who works miracles
and I only want a little miracle,
one he can do
while he's doing all the big ones.

"What I want is for him to magic everyone
here for Christmas Day:
Josie, Jamie, Raff, Conor, Beau.
The whole family
around the Christmas tree,
and brilliant presents for everyone,
wrapped in gold paper
with red Santas and flying reindeer.
I want it just like it was when I was young."

Tony Curtis

Christmas Sounds

Boeings wing softly over Earth
Humming like enormous *Messiahs*
Bringing everyone home for Christmas;

Children wailing impossible wants,
Housewives worrying in case enough isn't,
Parsons, with prevenient care, sucking Strepsils,

Telly jingling twinkling mistletoe-ing,
Cash tills recording glad tidings of profit,
Office parties munching through menus –

Crackers! Champagne corks!

At the heart of it all, in the hay,
No sound at all but the cattle
Endlessly chewing it over.

UA Fanthorpe (1929 – 2009)

The Carol of the Stable

The stable was warm and the stable was dry,
The night was so cold when a robin flew by.
'Is there shelter,' she asked, 'from the fierce winter roar?'
'Come in,' said the stable. 'There is room for one more.'

The robin flew in and was perched in the hay,
When a hungry young field mouse was passing that way.
'Do you happen to have any scraps in your store?'
'Come in,' said the stable. 'There is room for one more.'

As the field mouse sat nibbling a stray ear of wheat,
A lost, lonely fox staggered in from the street.
He looked worn-out and haggard as he stood in the door,
'Come in,' said the stable. 'There is room for one more.'

To the warmth of the stable while the fox rested there,
From across the wide valley there came a brown hare.
Her back leg was bleeding, she was hungry and sore,
'Come in,' said the stable. 'There is room for one more.'

Came a cat with her kittens who were left in the snow,
Then a bitch and her litter who had nowhere to go.
A cow and her calf wandered in from the cold,
And a ewe with her lamb who had strayed from their fold.

The birds flew from the forests and up from the glen,
The chaffinch and sparrow, the blackbird and wren.
But no matter how many would come to the door,
The stable said, 'Welcome. There is room for one more.'

Till an old weary donkey stood waiting outside,
'We've had such a long journey and have nowhere to bide.'
From his ears to his tail, he was covered in hoar,
'Come in,' said the stable. 'There is room for one more.'

Then into the stable he carried his load,
The load he had guarded along Bethlehem's road.
'My lady must rest now. Her baby is due.'
'Come in,' said the stable. 'We've been waiting for you.'

Bill Adair

Carol of the Three Kings

How long ago we dreamed
Evening and the human
Step in the quiet groves
And the prayer we said:
Walk upon the darkness,
Words of the lord,
Contain the night, the dead
And here comfort us.
We have been a shadow
Many nights moving,
Swaying many nights
Between yes and no.
We have been blindness
Between sun and moon
Coaxing the time
For a doubtful star.
Now we cease, we forget
Our reasons, our city,
The sun, the perplexed day,
Noon, the irksome labor,
The flushed dream, the way,
Even the dark beasts,
Even our shadows.
In this night and day
All gifts are nothing:
What is frankincense
Where all sweetness is?
We that were followers
In the night's confusion
Kneel and forget our feet
Who the cold way came.
Now in the darkness
After the deep song
Walk among the branches
Angels of the lord,
Over earth and child
Quiet the boughs.

Now shall we sing or pray?
Where has the night gone?
Who remembers day?
We are breath and human
And awake have seen
All birth and burial
Merge and fall away,
Seen heaven that extends
To comfort all the night,
We have felt morning move
The grove of a few hands.

WS Merwin (1927 – 2019)

Christmas Pudding

Richness waits under spare beds,
at the back of fridges. The more cautious
have placed theirs at the bottom of freezers.

Made according to family recipes,
passed down or across to new recruits –
a whole day's steaming takes commitment.

My Auntie Jean, whose Welsh recipe I follow,
always ensured her grandchildren stopped by
on mixing day to stir and make a wish.

Last November I stirred in hope
in my mother's kitchen and kidded myself
it wouldn't just be the two of us for dinner.

We hid it away in her overflow freezer –
she always has enough food on hand to feed
her four grown-up children at a moment's notice.

It will be taken out on Christmas Eve.
As the jewels of fruit defrost maybe we will unthaw
a little ourselves, the kernels of two years'

disappointment and loss melting away.
My nephew will be old enough this year
to have a taste. But before the eating,

the dousing. I will try not to look
at the pudding's blue flame but the faces
gathered and lit around the table.

Lorraine Mariner

Christmas Dinner

Love sounds like noise,
a conversation, a chiming in, a chatter

of many voices brought together, and in between
the noise, silence sings its part im-

perfectly, missing beats or interrupting,
never reaching a final note. There's always

a codetta or a ritornello, one last message you promised
to pass on, someone you meant to speak to, a sound

that makes you look up, and say: I must just
see who's arrived. Love is knocking on the door,

love is pulling up a chair, love is tapping on the side of its glass,
love opens many mouths and starts to sing:

Corinna Keefe

Born This Happy Morning

Put her in a chair by the fire where she can see
the decorations. She loves her food, turkey,
the trimmings. We have to face it though,
she doesn't know who we are any more.

Look Mum, there's that fairy you made for the tree,
its skirt's come loose, we used to fight
over who would put it at the top.....
She loves the carols, we could have a singalong

From a faraway room she hears voices,
the shadow of laughter on a wall,
one long Christmas dinner, people
hark the herald gloria in excelsis

reproducing themselves, years, leaves fluttering.
That boy there with the slender neck stalk
did she marry him or bath him
away in a manger

or was he the one waiting for her at the bus stop?
She knows she loves him. She doesn't believe
we know who she is
or who we are but at least we're together

meringue explodes softly into a white moustache
she's always had a sweet tooth
and they are singing
as she loses her place in the air

but her fingers still nimble, tying
lost threads round the Christmas tree fairy.
Eyes close, candlelight strokes her face
and oh the Christmas tree, the sparkle of it

then awake, searching, as if she could find
her way home in the depth of her family's eyes.
Her sister hugs the hoop of her shrunken body
sing in exultation

They hold hands and sing it again
joyful and triumphant
and from the chair a full throated blast, a shout

triumphant.

Christina Buckton

A Christmas dinner plate with the pattern still visible

We need a pan for the Brussels sprouts, not that one
the one underneath, another for the potatoes.
The kettle's boiling, open a window:
maybe it's better with no one in the kitchen:
there's the table to lay now the cooking's begun.

I need to divide the sausages,
twist them in their skins
and snip them apart ready to roast:
one each and some left over.

When I was a girl, I used to run upstairs,
a half cooked turkey skidding in the pan,
its side peppered with skewer marks,
to ask my mother if the juices were running clear.
Then back down to the oven for another hour or so
pulling the door closed with a lifted latch,
my mother turned under a quilt
in a darkened room,
while I basted the bird with cloudy fat.

We're getting on: the kitchen rattles and fumes,
a saucepan of potatoes overflows a brown scum.
Turn the gas down, maybe pour some wine.

When my grandparents were alive
we used to start with grapefruit.
My father had the curved knife
but we cut between segments.
There were old pink cherries
to fish out of a jar with a spoon.
It is always at this time of year
the snow fails to come
and, more recently, it has rained for several days.
But it's nearly always dark,
so we close the curtains, light candles,
roll roast potatoes with a fork, in spitting fat,

find somewhere to warm the plates:
we're not used to cooking for such a crowd.

This year again we have glazed carrots
with butter, sugar and cinnamon;
it reminds me of mulled wine.

It's strange how the air seems to empty
as we carry in the food:
how the table shrinks
until we're elbow to elbow,
yet it never seems that everyone is there;
as though somewhere, in another room
great aunts and uncles,
grandparents we can barely now remember,
sit patiently with empty sherry glasses
waiting to be called through.

The children squint down their crackers,
they don't like the bang but they want a paper hat
even though it'll be too big,
and maybe a piece of bright plastic that spins
or a jangle of puzzle rings.

Pass round the dishes if you can,
the sprouts are a bit overcooked
but the potatoes are all right, maybe next year.
Is everybody happy,
are all the glasses full? Then let's begin.

Kate Bass

Playing Love Hangover While Washing Up

for Ava

If there's a cure for this –
I'm steeping my wrists in bubbles tonight,
a twentieth century girl
reeling to seventies disco, when Diana
swoops her crazy laugh.
This first Christmas without Helen
I could work out how she might endure.

In a pewter snowflake
dangling from a tree; in the heads
of friends, or that parallel moment
when she drags on a fag and it never ends.
I could welcome my grand-daughter, a month
into her first breaths. What might I promise
Ava? She'll find giraffes and pomegranates,
cafés and politicians, damaged magnolias,
floods and forest fires, make friends who could
last nearly a lifetime.

Before I dipped these saucepans
I looped two red ribbons and two grey snowflakes
over a fir-tree's bristles, thinking *one for each
lost friend*, sipping sherry, hearing Judy sing
we'll have to muddle through somehow, as if
muddling becomes its own answer.
Go Judy and Diana – give me longing
between the branches, soapsuds after
the sherry, a clatter of forks, when I rinse
once more the innocent face of a plate.

If there's a cure for this I don't want it –
my missing quartet of friends, my grand-daughter
dreaming, my twenty-first century girl.
How can I hold them all in my hands
without overflowing, while a cat laps

urgently at water, and rain tonight
wrestles away from the sea? Let it fall
like a fork or snowflake:
this unfinished welcome, this swirling song.

Robert Hamberger

Boxing Day at my Grandparents' House

Gathering up most of the festivities
- leftover turkey, Christmas pudding,
Turkish delight, Snowballs, cherries

 - we were like a family of snails,
transporting our home to theirs,
spiral shells packed with glad tidings.

My mother trooped us up the path,
balancing a boozy trifle on one hand
and a foil covered plate on the other.

Tasked with carrying spare cutlery
in his rucksack, my brother jingled
as he flew his Millennium Falcon

across the lawn, firing lasers at the ice
in the bird bath. As always, I dawdled
behind him, Pound Puppy strapped

to my back, bestowing imaginary wings
on Grumpy Care Bear and wheeling
Barbie's campervan to the waiting

feet of my grandma. Assigned only
sweets and new toys, I dangled tinsel
from various pockets, a glistening trail

for my dad who had the heaviest load:
a colour television. It was tradition.
Just for this one day, my grandparents

wanted Maria von Trapp and Salzburg
in Austrian shades and those one-off
specials in the warm hues of the season.

My dad held this box like the gift it was,
careful not to drop it, or even tilt it –
making us believe Julie Andrews herself

would tumble out, swiftly followed by
Fred Astaire, then Morecambe and Wise –
all dancing their way to the front door.

Jeanette Burton

Christmas in Benalmádena

What are we hiding
when we open someone else's door

Outside
the sea the sand the village
you and I and the mountain

Inside
laughter by a fireplace
a letter full of commas
a tray of turrón
and a guest telling another guest –
touch the door where your lover lived
touch the handle where you placed
your grief for the first time
touch the flame that meant
something to you

Isn't that what happens in celebration –
hearts move in windows?

Nathalie Handal

Afterword

Afterword

Being together and looking after each other. Whatever the time of year, what could be more important, particularly after the last couple of years we have all faced? Christmas, however, creates those special moments and memories that can last a lifetime and beyond.

The poems in this pamphlet will provide comfort and joy to many. The opening poem by one of Vicky McClure's Our Dementia Choir members, Maureen Richardson, has a poignant tale to tell of her childhood and the memories made with her family at a special time.

Maureen sadly passed away last year after living with dementia for a number of years. We were proud to have her as a member of the choir and remember fondly her times singing with the choir.

Our Dementia Choir is one big family; supporting, caring and looking out for each other. After almost three years, the choir is still going strong and the commitment and togetherness of this fabulous group is invaluable to those living with dementia. People living with this dreadful disease – both the individual and their carers and families – can be experiencing a living bereavement as you lose the person you love day by day. But having people around, being together and remembering times gone past is so important for them.

Thank you to Candlestick Press for nominating Vicky McClure's Dementia Choir as their chosen charity for this pamphlet – it will support the togetherness we all share as a choir family.

Karen Bonser, Charity Manager and wife of Mick Bonser, 54, Our Dementia Choir member living with early onset dementia

Our Dementia Choir is exactly that, "Ours": somewhere families can all come together, support one another with a connected bond in our happy place filled with music.

Vicky McClure